The Classical Piano
Sheet Music Series

INTERMEDIATE
ROMANTIC ERA
FAVORITES

ISBN 978-1-5400-8903-8

HAL•LEONARD®

Visit Hal Leonard Online at
www.halleonard.com

Contact us:
Hal Leonard
7777 West Bluemound Road
Milwaukee, WI 53213
Email: info@halleonard.com

In Europe, contact:
Hal Leonard Europe Limited
42 Wigmore Street
Marylebone, London, W1U 2RN
Email: info@halleonardeurope.com

In Australia, contact:
Hal Leonard Australia Pty. Ltd.
4 Lentara Court
Cheltenham, Victoria, 3192 Australia
Email: info@halleonard.com.au

Contents

Gavotte in D Minor
from *Children's Album*

Amy Marcy Beach
Op. 36, No. 2

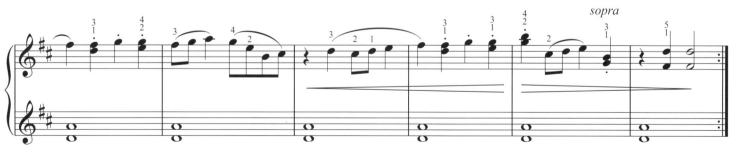

Fingerings are from the first edition.

Waltz in A-flat Major

Johannes Brahms
1833–1897
Op. 39, No. 15

Moderate Waltz tempo

Ballade
from *25 Easy and Progressive Studies*

Johann Friedrich Burgmüller
1806–1874
Op. 100, No. 15

Allegro con brio (♩. = 104)

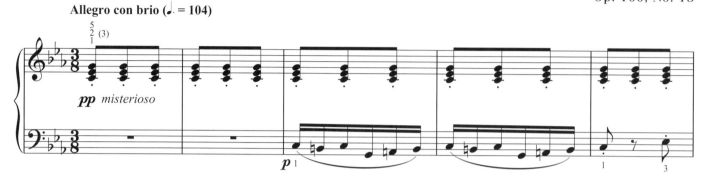

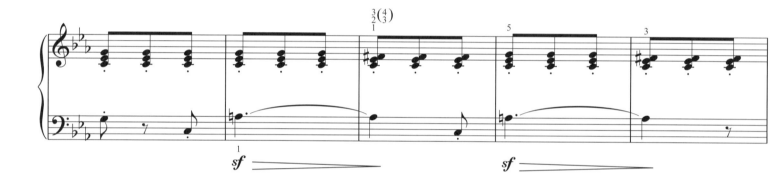

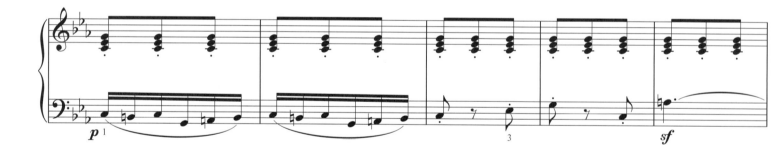

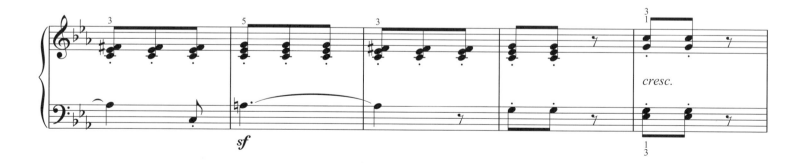

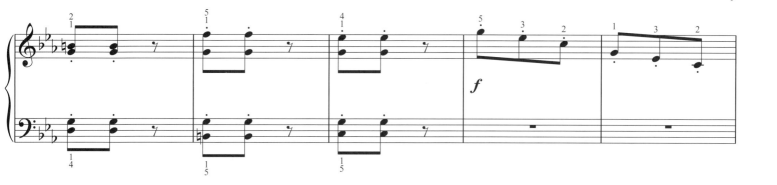

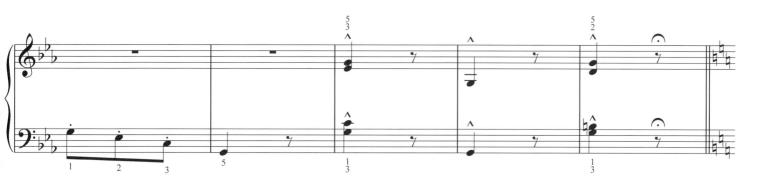

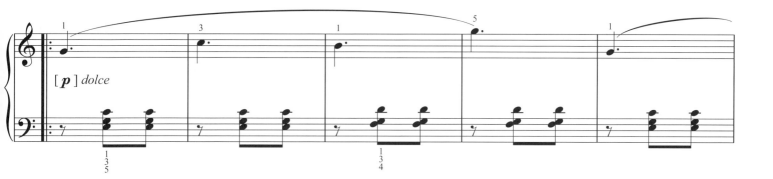

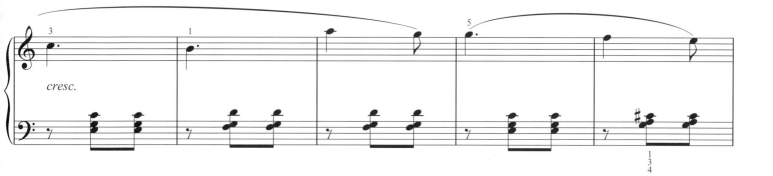

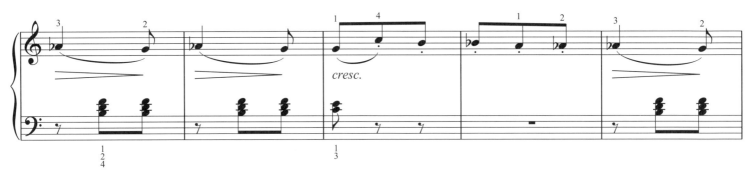

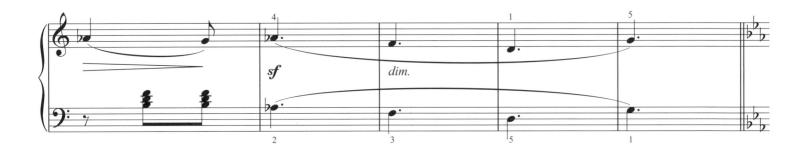

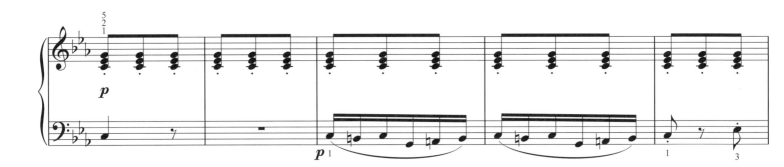

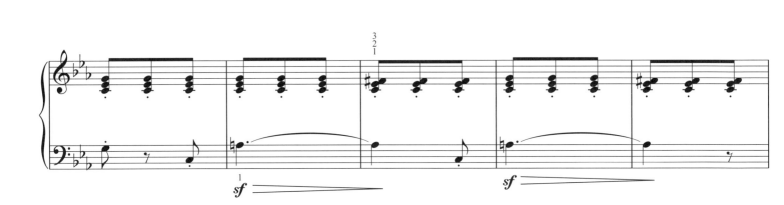

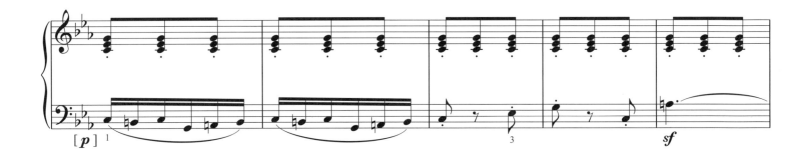

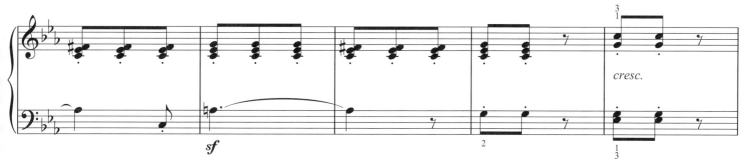

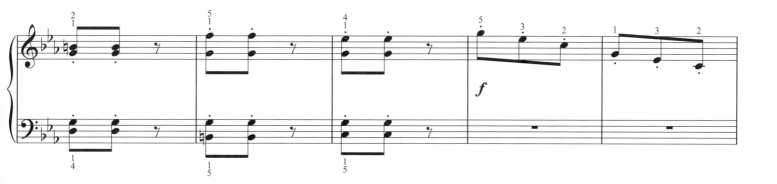

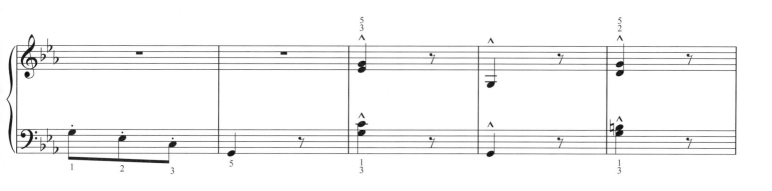

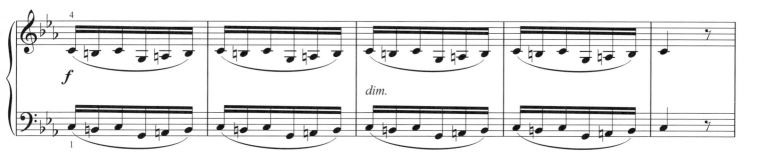

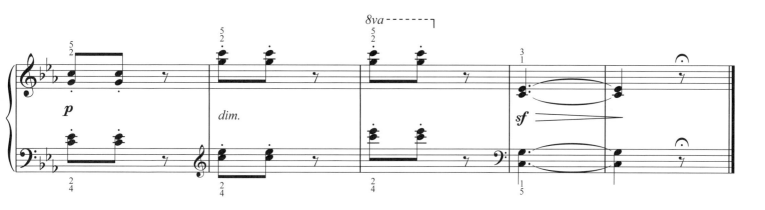

Confidence

from *18 Characteristic Studies*
(18 Études de genre)

Johann Friedrich Burgmüller
1806–1874
Op. 109, No. 1

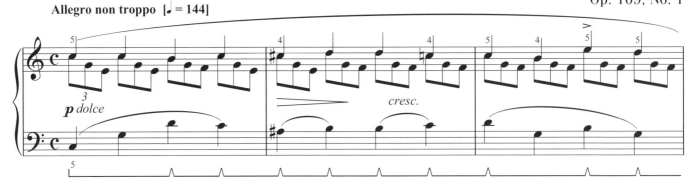

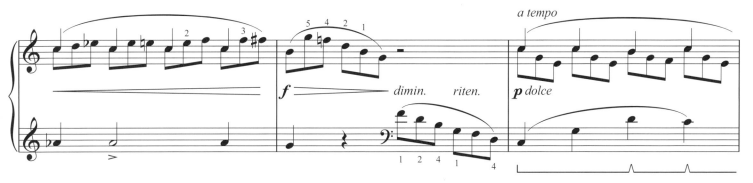

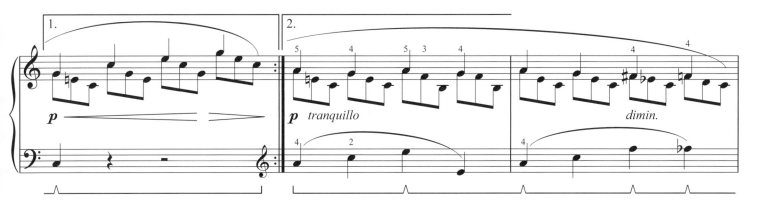

Restlessness
(Inquiétude)
from *25 Easy and Progressive Studies*

Johann Friedrich Burgmüller
1806–1874
Op. 100, No. 18

Allegro agitato (♩ = 138)

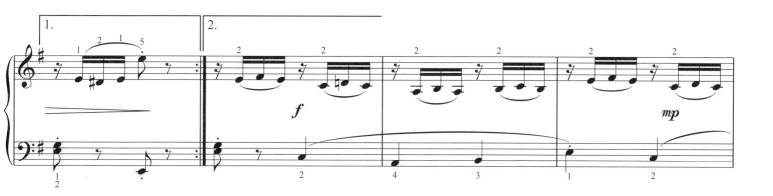

Sincerity
(La Candeur)
from *25 Easy and Progressive Studies*

Johann Friedrich Burgmüller
1806–1874
Op. 100, No. 1

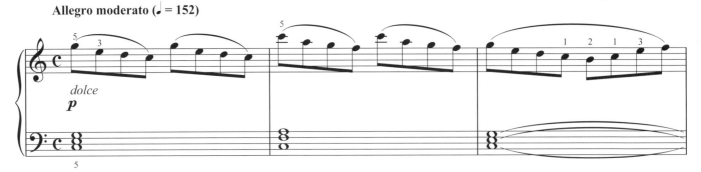

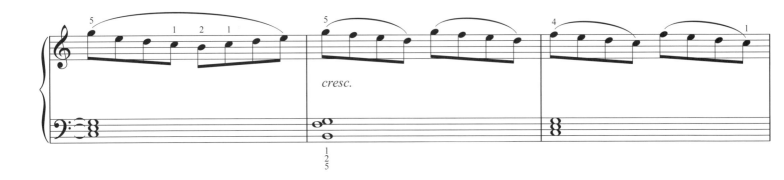

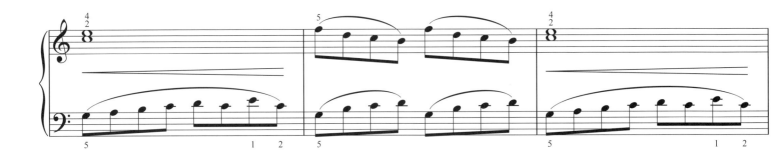

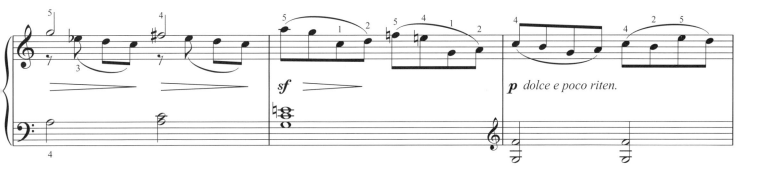

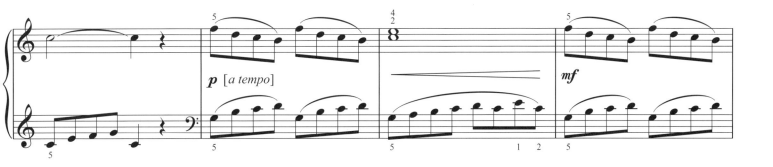

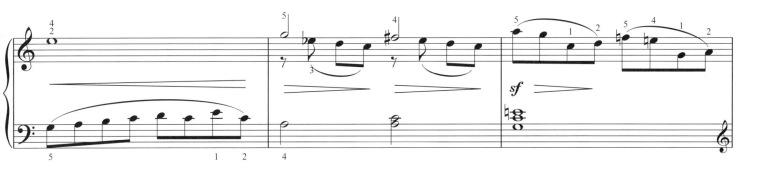

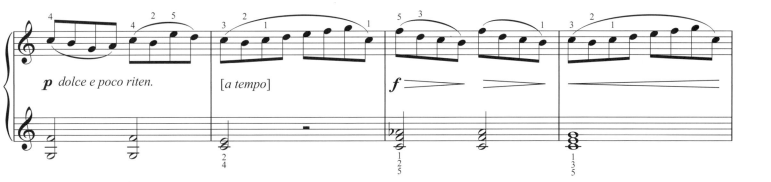

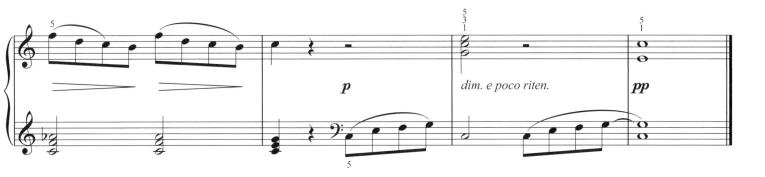

Mazurka in F Major

Frédéric Chopin
1810–1849
Op. 68, No. 3

Allegro ma non troppo

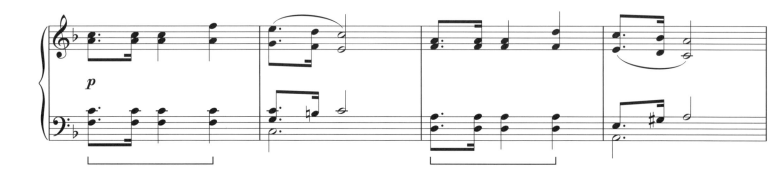

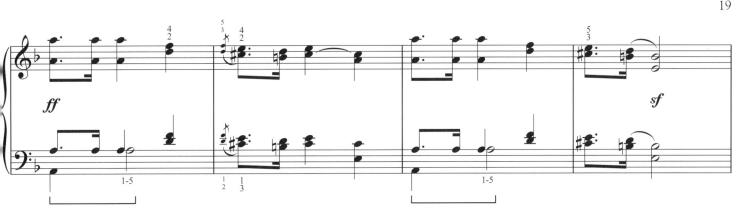

Poco più vivo

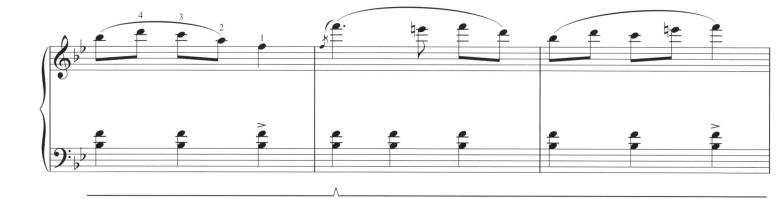

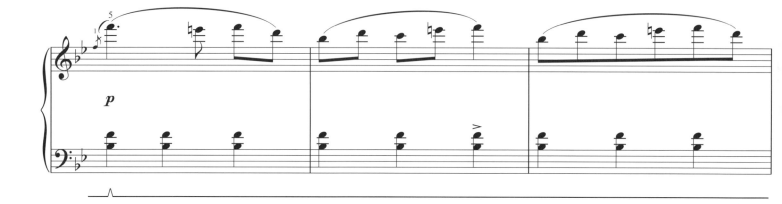

rit.

Tempo I

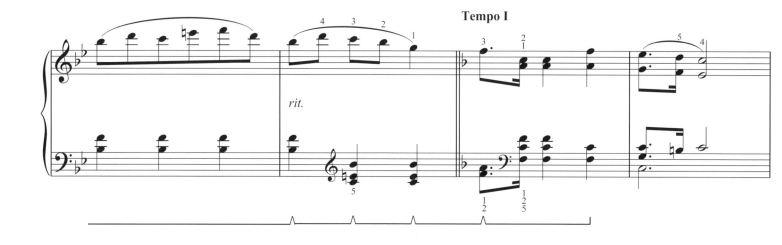

Prelude in E Minor

Frédéric Chopin
1810–1849
Op. 28, No. 4

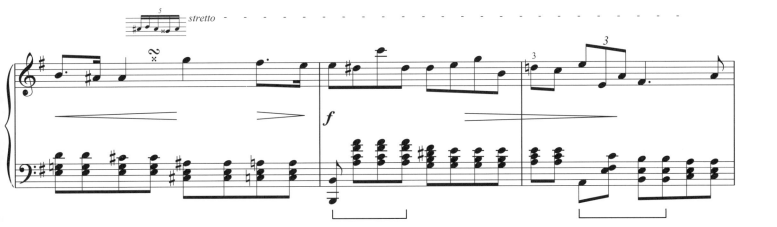

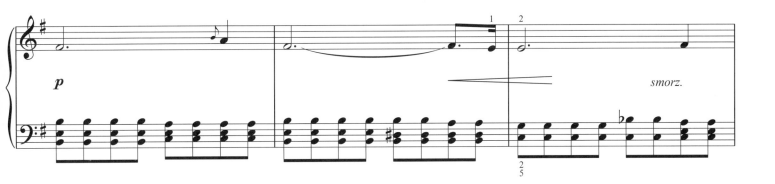

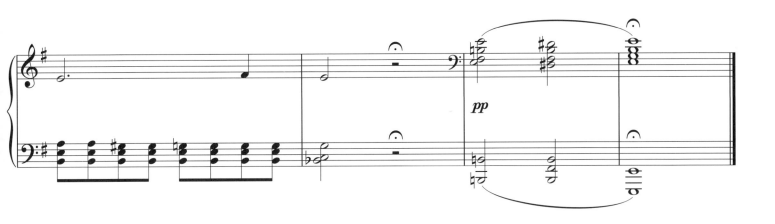

Prelude in B Minor

Frédéric Chopin
1810–1849
Op. 28, No. 6

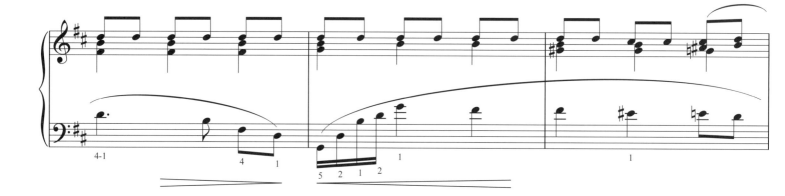

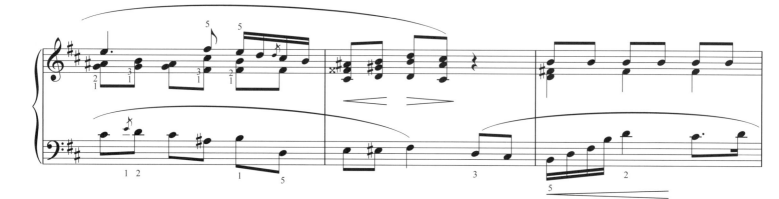

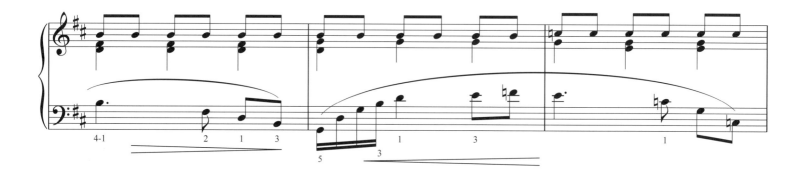

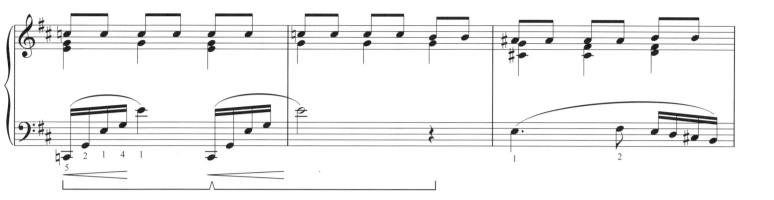

Prelude in D-flat Major
("Raindrop")

Frédéric Chopin
1810–1849
Op. 28, No. 15

Sostenuto [♩ = 63-72]

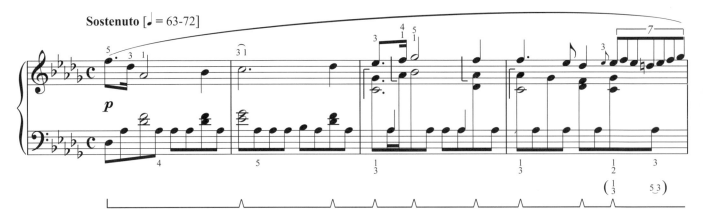

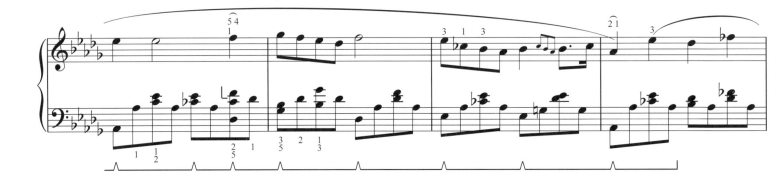

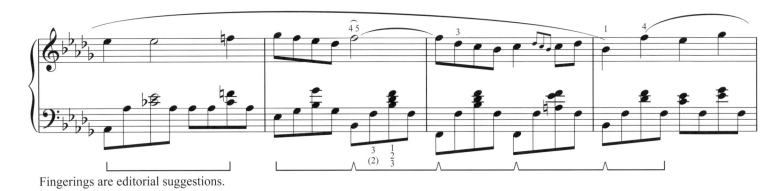

Fingerings are editorial suggestions.

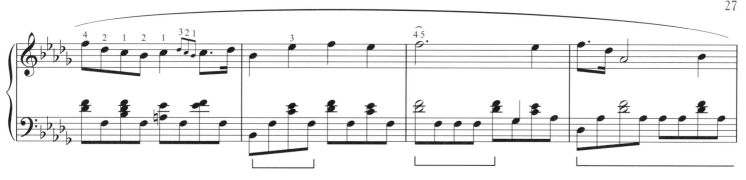

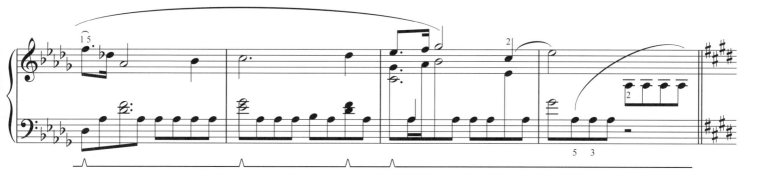

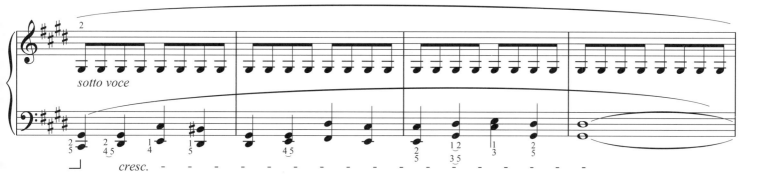

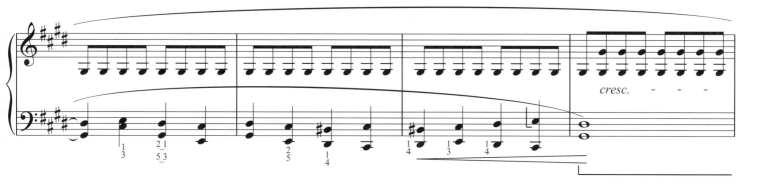

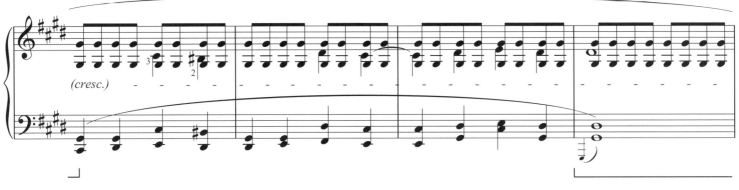

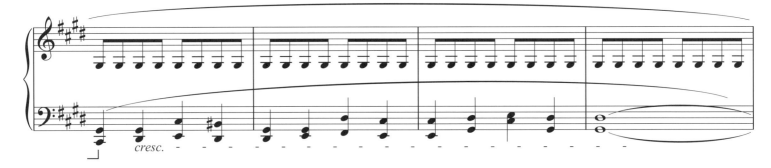

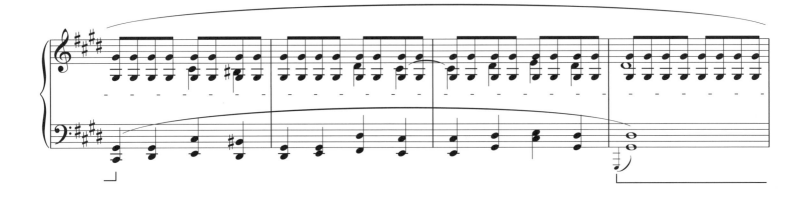

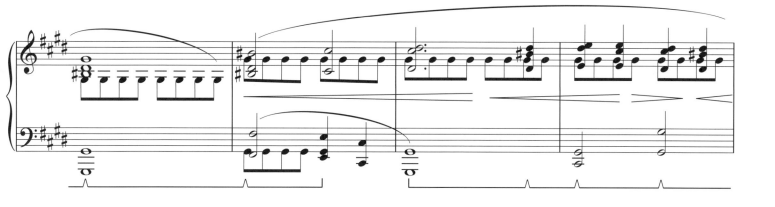

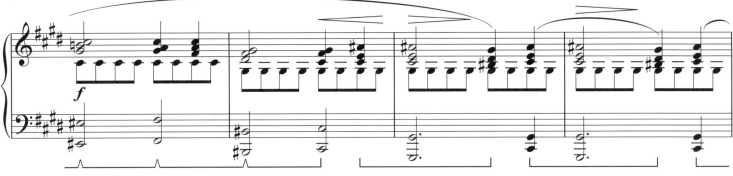

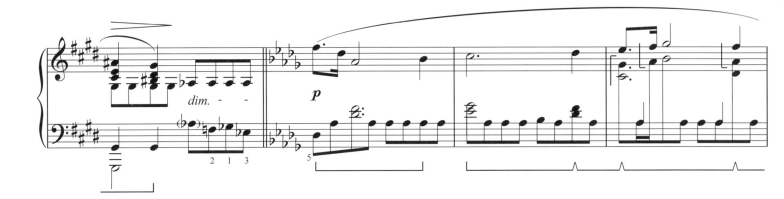

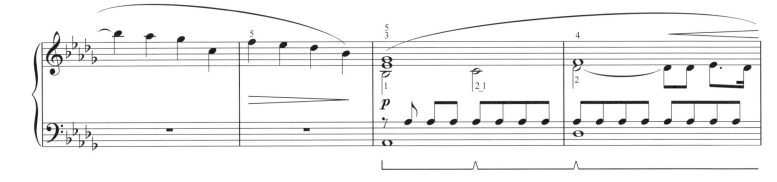

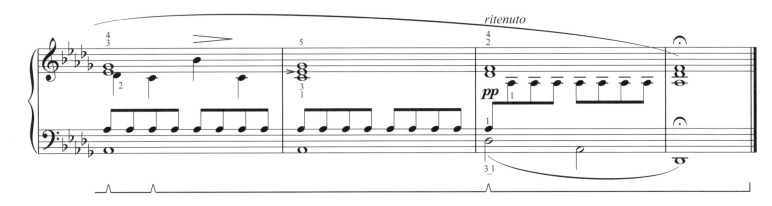

Spinning Song
from *Musical Character Pieces*

Albert Ellmenreich
1816–1905
Op. 14, No. 5

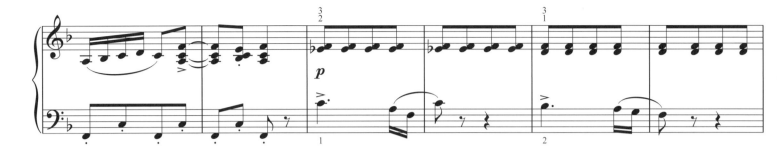

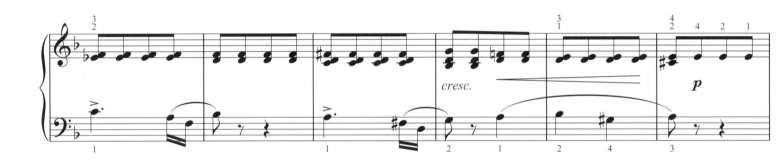

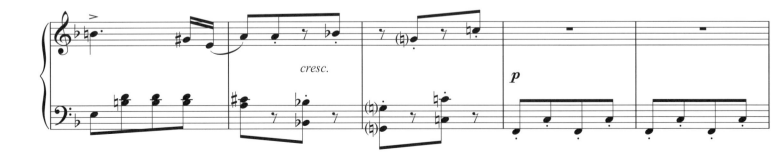

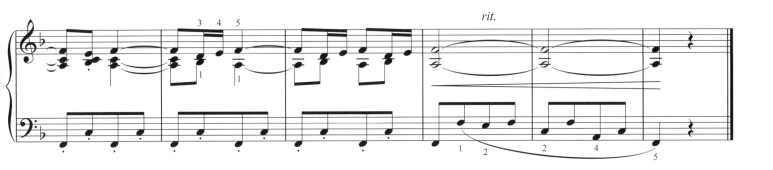

Arietta
from *Lyric Pieces*

Edvard Grieg
1843–1907
Op. 12, No. 1

Poco Andante e sostenuto

con pedale

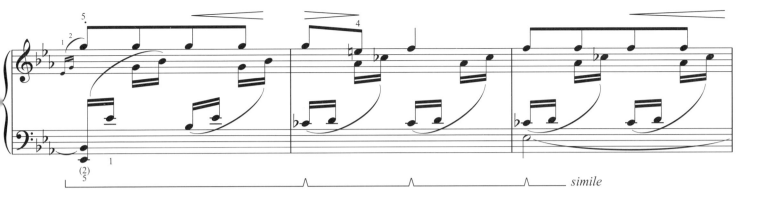

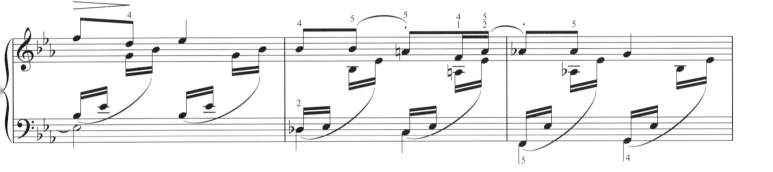

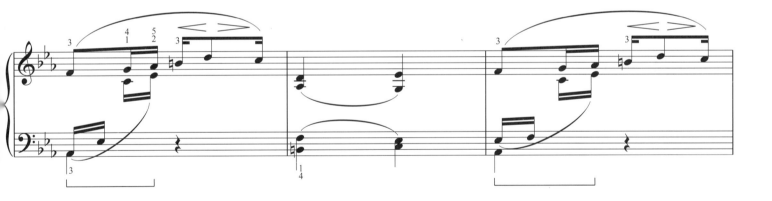

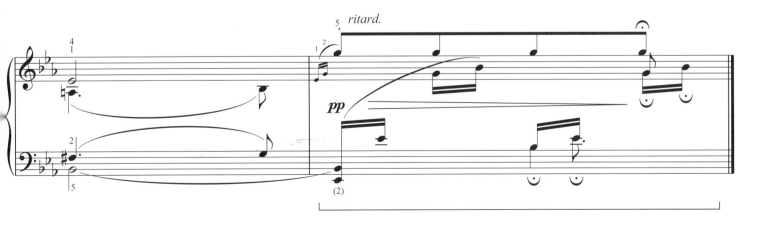

Waltz
from *Lyric Pieces*

Edvard Grieg
1843–1907
Op. 12, No. 2

Allegro moderato [♩. = 56]

simile

37

Dance of the Elves
(Elverdans)
from *Lyric Pieces*

Edvard Grieg
1843–1907
Op. 12, No. 4

Molto allegro e sempre staccato [♩. = 92–96]

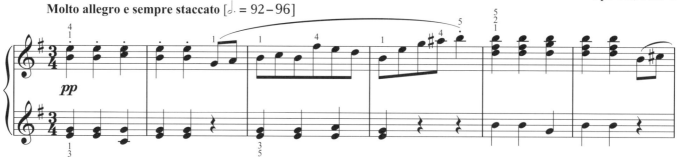

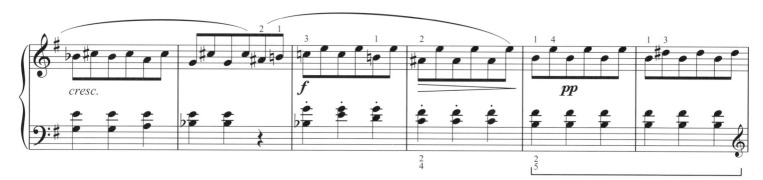

Solitary Traveler

(Ensom Vandrer)

from *Lyric Pieces*

Edvard Grieg
1843–1907
Op. 43, No. 2

Puck
from *Lyric Pieces*

Edvard Grieg
1843–1907
Op. 71, No. 3

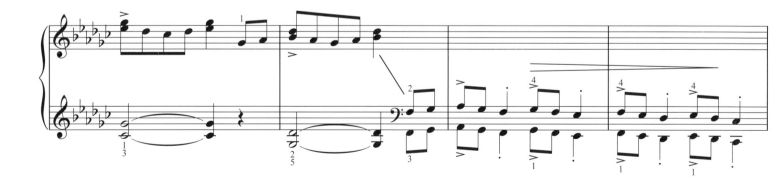

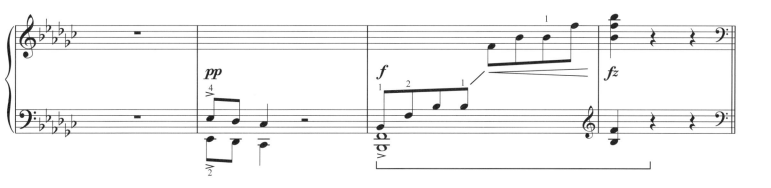

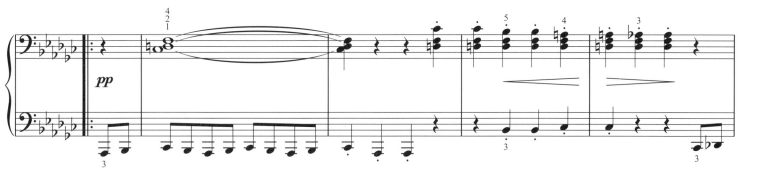

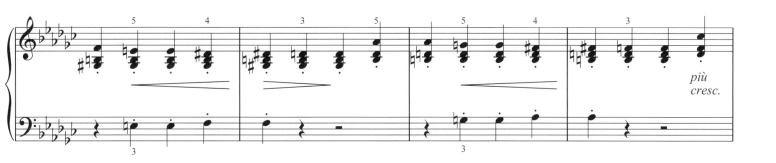

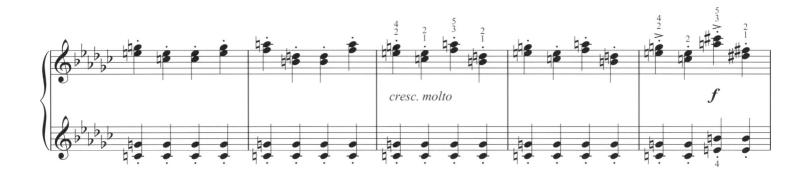

The Avalanche
from *25 Melodious Etudes*

Stephen Heller
1813–1888
Op. 45, No. 2

Allegro vivace [♩ = 92–96]

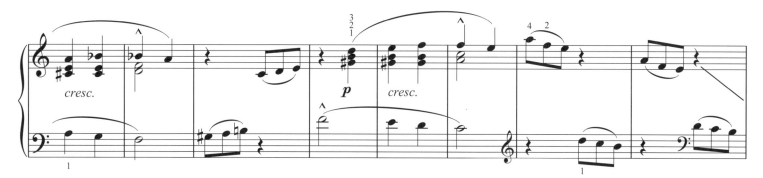

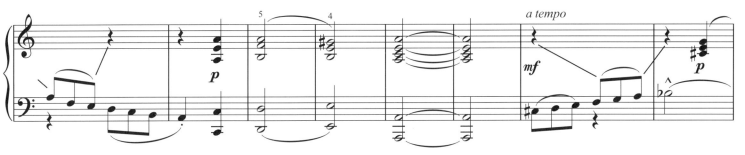

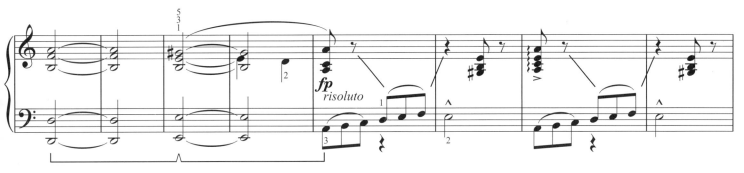

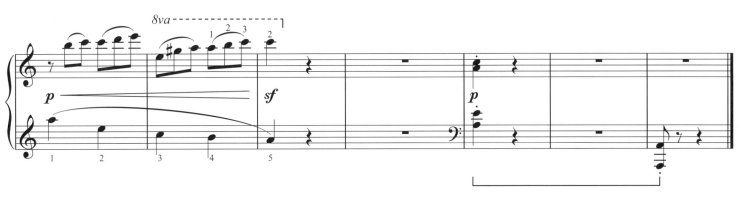

Allegretto
("Scampering")
from *25 Etudes*

Stephen Heller
1813–1888
Op. 47, No. 1

Allegretto (♩ = 80)

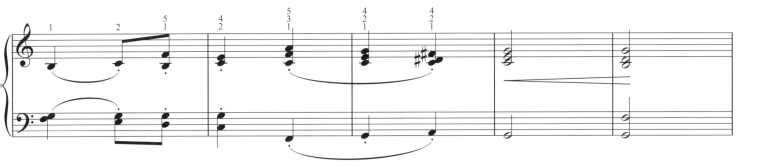

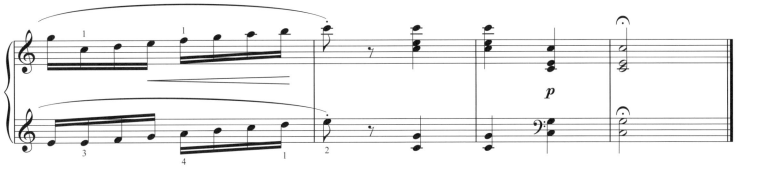

Grandmother Tells a Ghost Story

from *Scenes from Childhood*

Theodor Kullak
1818–1882
Op. 81, No. 3

Allegretto

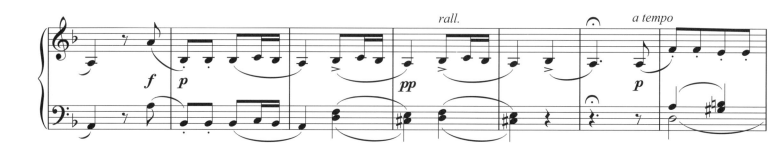

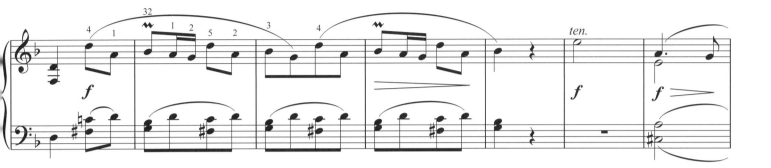

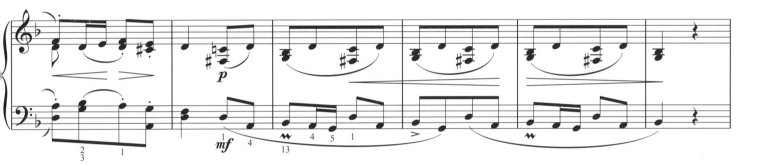

Grandmother
goes to sleep.

To a Wild Rose
from *Woodland Sketches*

Edward MacDowell
1860–1908
Op. 51, No. 1

With simple tenderness (♩ = 88)

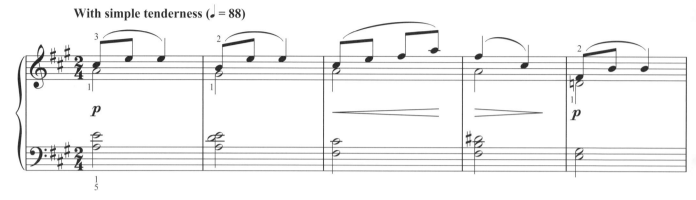

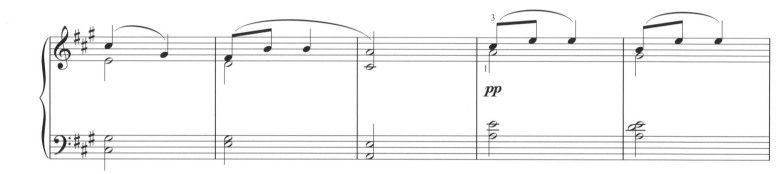

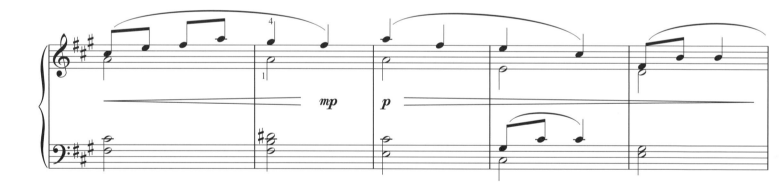

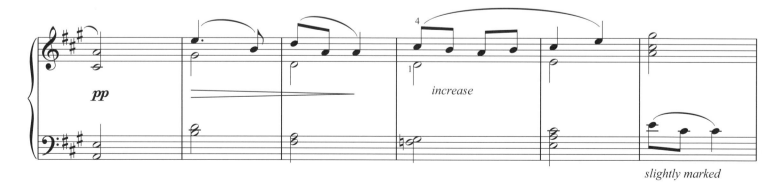

slightly marked

still increase

f diminish   rit.

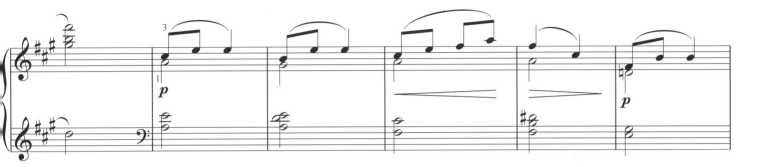

p

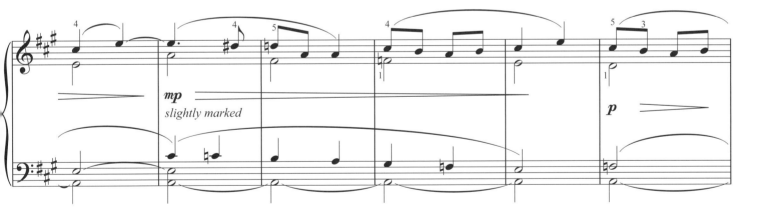

mp
slightly marked

p

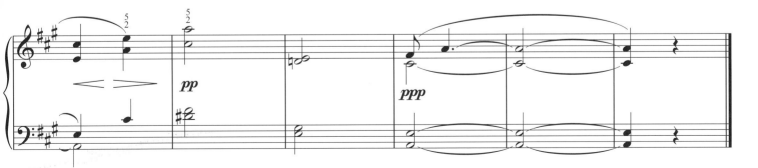

pp

ppp

Consolation
from *Songs Without Words*

Felix Mendelssohn
1809–1847
Op. 30, No. 3

Adagio non troppo

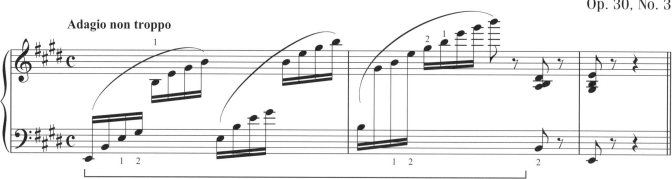

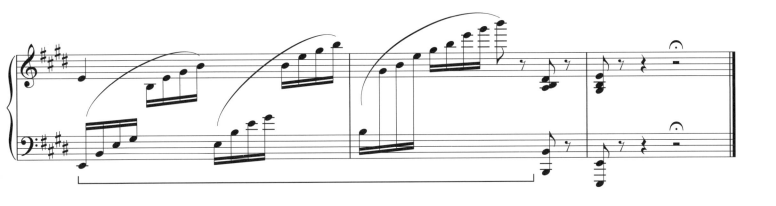

Folk Melody
(Im Volkston)
from *Five Piano Pieces*

Carl Nielsen
1865–1931
Op. 3, No. 1

* Literally "humming" in Danish. It is unclear what the composer intends.

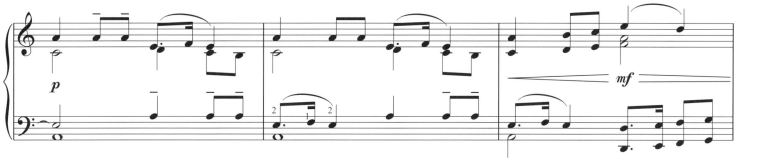

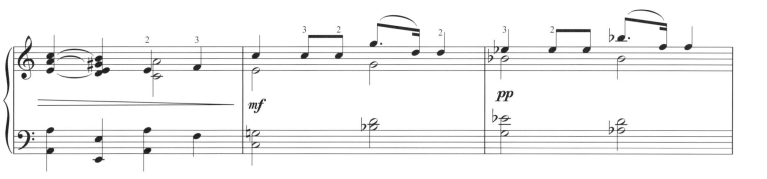

Waltz in B Minor

Franz Schubert
1797–1828
D. 145 (Op. 18, No. 6)

[Allegro moderato]

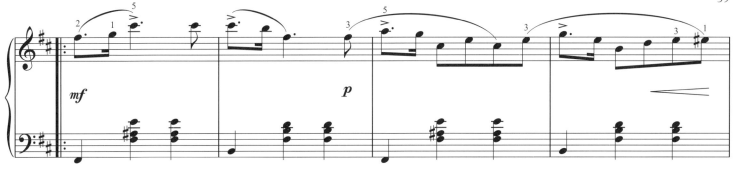

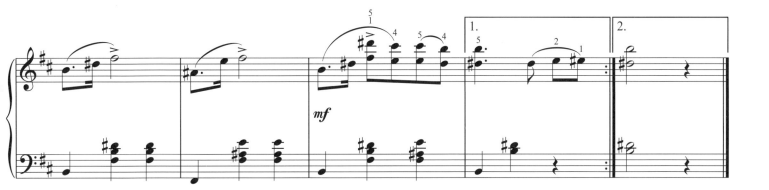

Waltz in A-flat Major

Franz Schubert
1797–1828
Op. 9, No. 12 (D. 365)

Allegretto e dolce

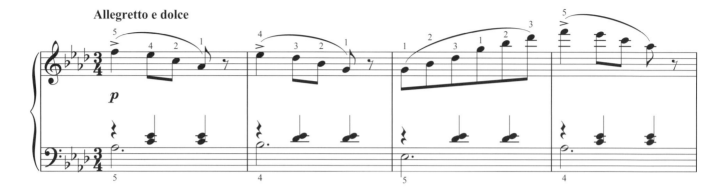

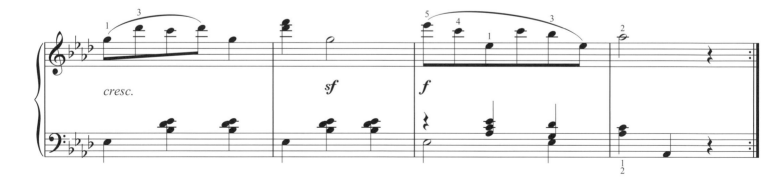

Of Strange Lands and People
(Von fremden Ländern und Menschen)
from *Scenes from Childhood*

Robert Schumann
1810–1856
Op. 15, No. 1

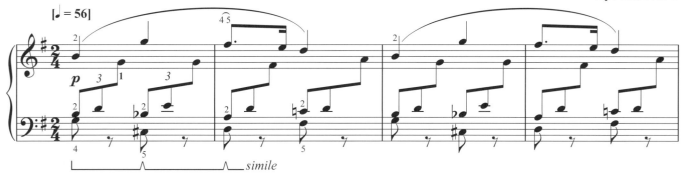

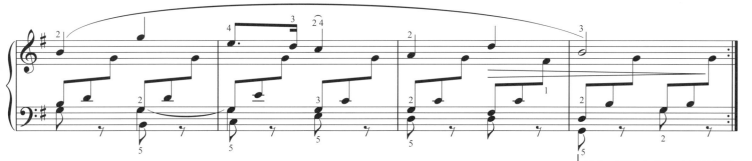

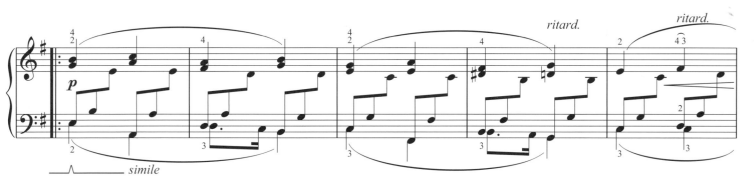

Träumerei
(Reverie)
from *Scenes from Childhood*

By Robert Schumann
1810–1856
Op. 15, No. 7

Slowly (♩ = 69)

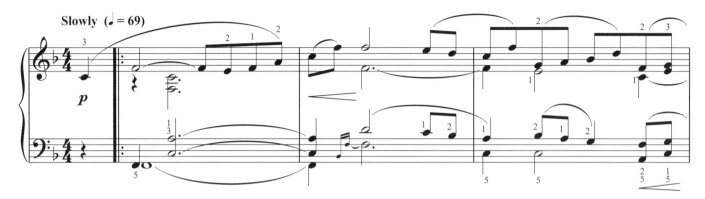

ritardando

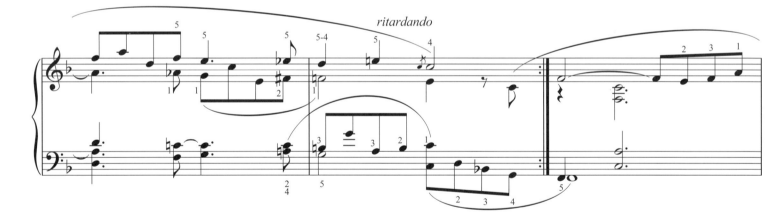

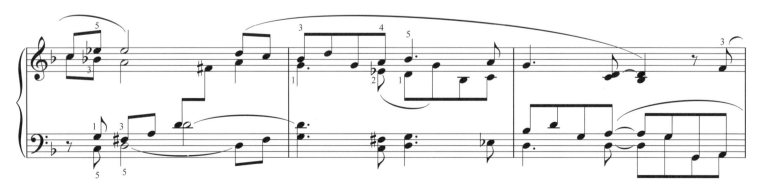

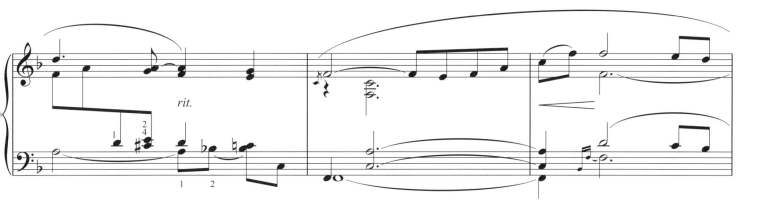

An Important Event
(Wichtige Begebenheit)
from *Scenes from Childhood*

By Robert Schumann
1810–1856
Op. 15, No. 6

Allegro marziale (♩ = 120)

Melody
(Melodie)
from *Album for the Young*

Robert Schumann
1810–1856
Op. 68, No. 1

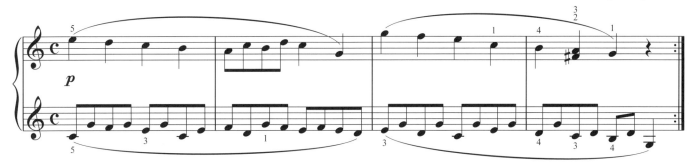

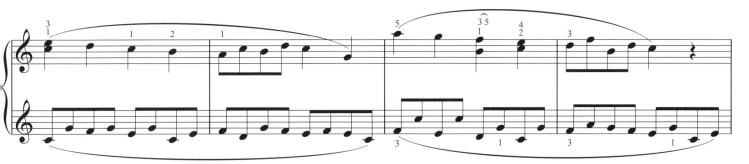

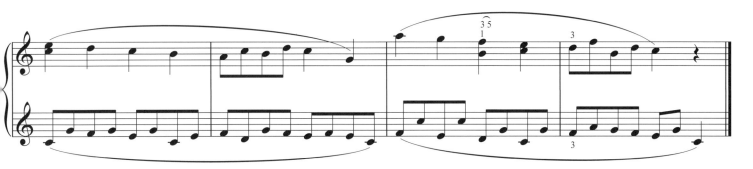

Soldiers' March
(Soldatenmarsch)
from *Album for the Young*

Robert Schumann
1810–1856
Op. 68, No. 2

Munter und straff
Lively and strict

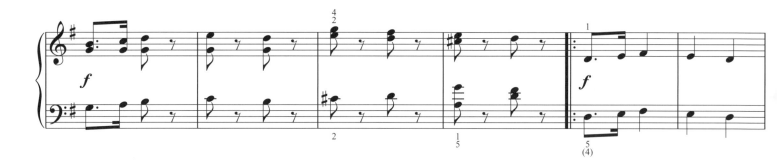

Humming Song
(Trällerliedchen)
from *Album for the Young*

Robert Schumann
1810–1856
Op. 68, No. 3

Nicht schnell
Not fast

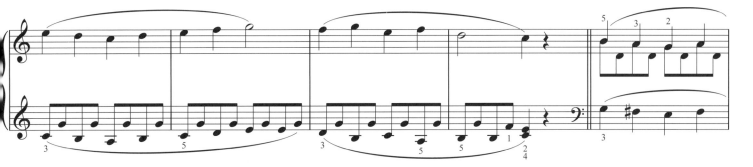

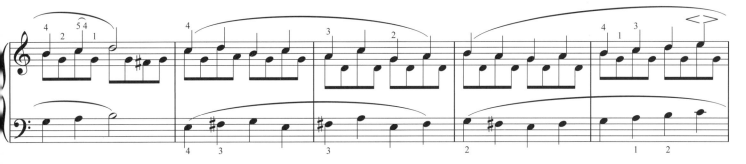

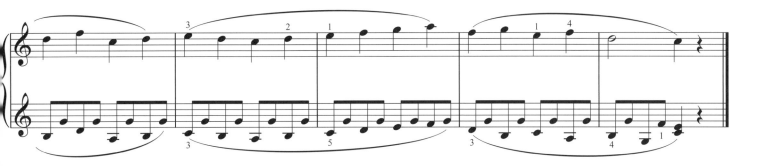

Little Piece
(Stückchen)
from *Album for the Young*

Robert Schumann
1810–1856
Op. 68, No. 5

Nicht schnell
Not fast

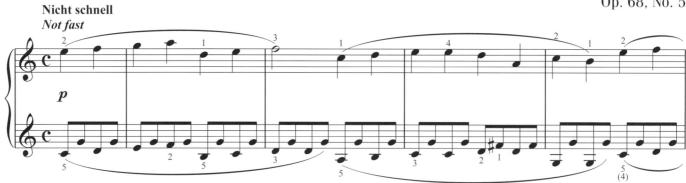

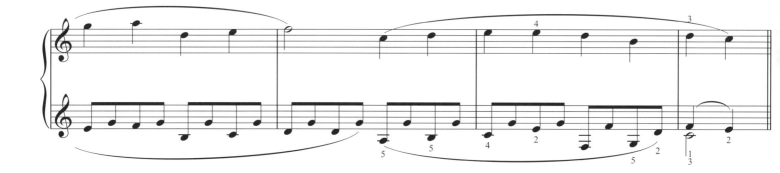

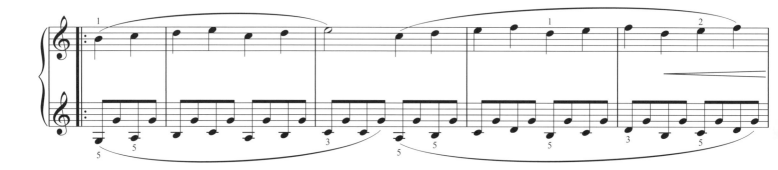

Hunting Song
(Jägerliedchen)
from *Album for the Young*

Robert Schumann
1810–1856
Op. 68, No. 7

Frisch und fröhlich
Briskly and merrily

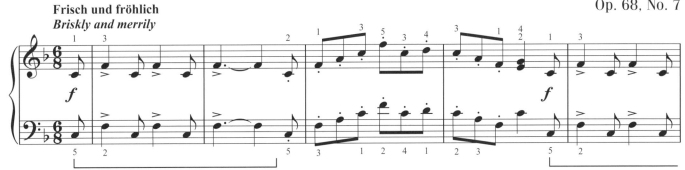

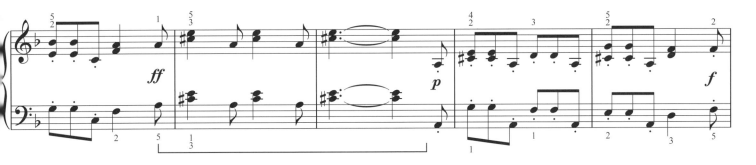

The Wild Horseman
(Wilder Reiter)
from *Album for the Young*

Robert Schumann
1810–1856
Op. 68, No. 8

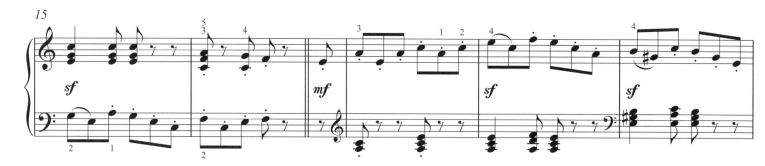

The Happy Farmer Returning from Work

(Fröhlicher Landmann, ven der Arbeit zurückkehrend)
from *Album for the Young*

Robert Schumann
1810–1856
Op. 68, No. 10

Frisch und munter
Brisk and lively

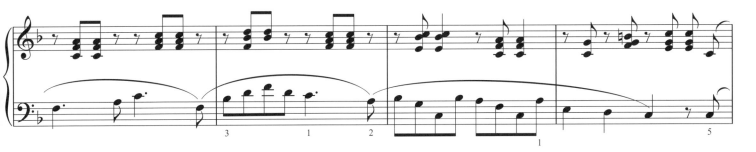

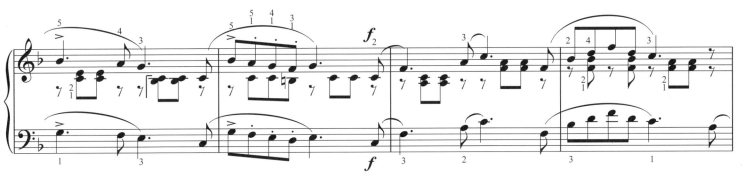

Little Study
(Kleine Studie)
from *Album for the Young*

Robert Schumann
1810–1856
Op. 68, No. 14

Leise und sehr egal zu spielen
Lightly and very evenly

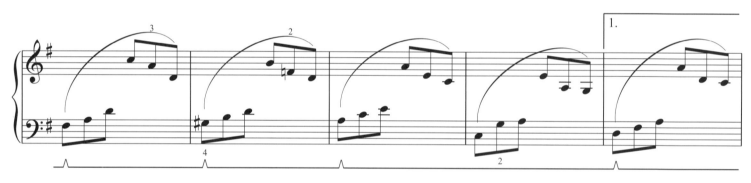

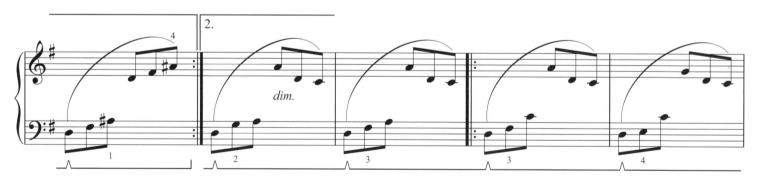

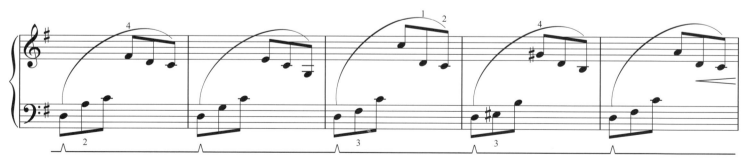

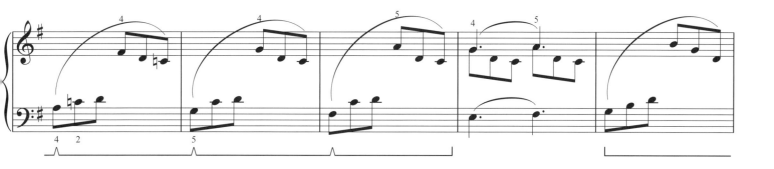

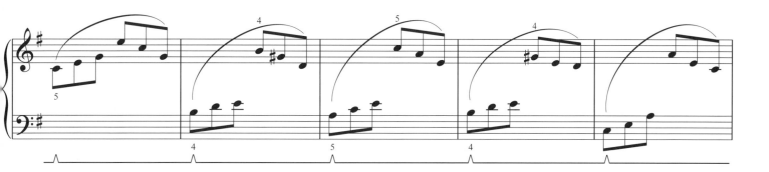

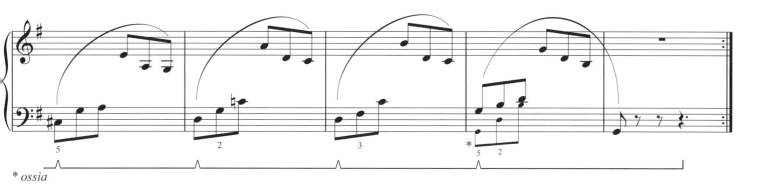

ossia

First Loss

(Erster Verlust)

from *Album for the Young*

Robert Schumann
1810–1856
Op. 68, No. 16

Nicht schnell
Not fast

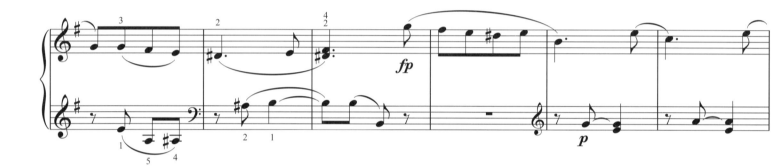

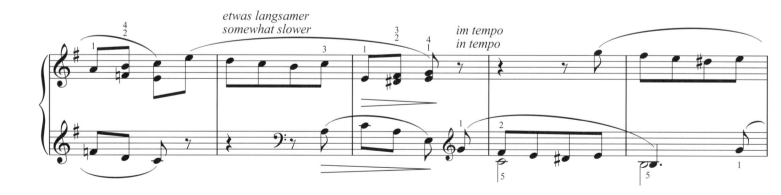

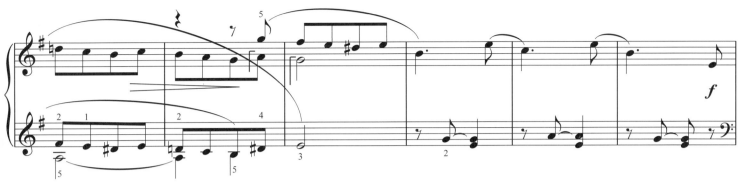

etwas langsamer
somewhat slower

im tempo
in tempo

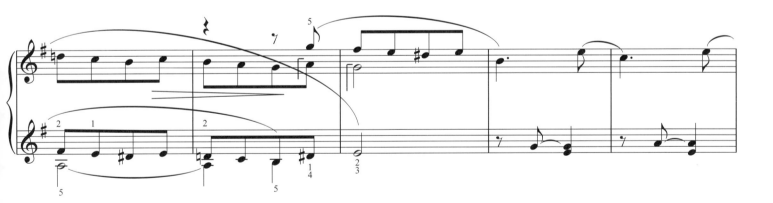

The Reaper's Song
(Schnitterliedchen)
from *Album for the Young*

Robert Schumann
1810–1856
Op. 68, No. 18

Nicht sehr schnell
Not very fast

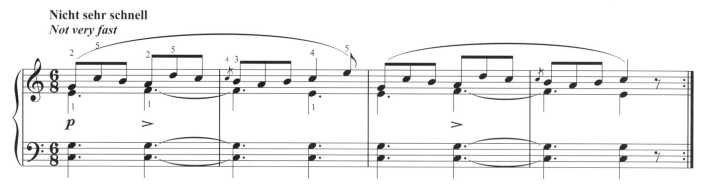

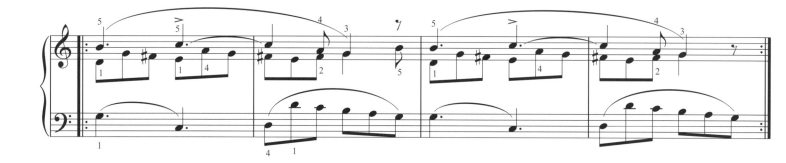

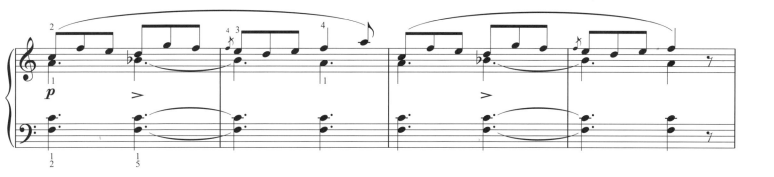

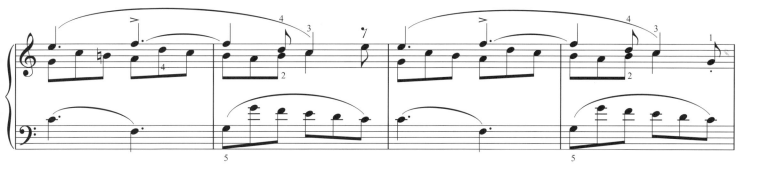

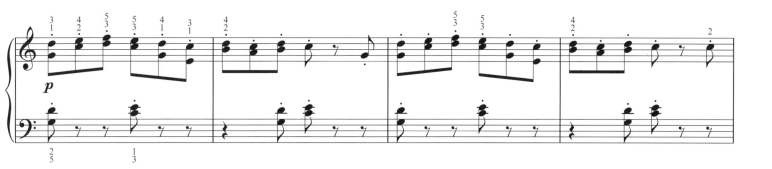

Mamma
from *Album for the Young*

Pyotr Il'yich Tchaikovsky
1840–1893
Op. 39, No. 4

Moderate (♩ = 88-92)

p with much feeling and tenderness

legatissimo

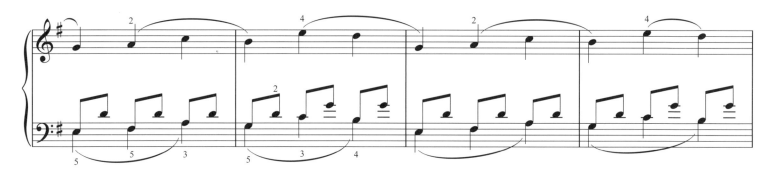

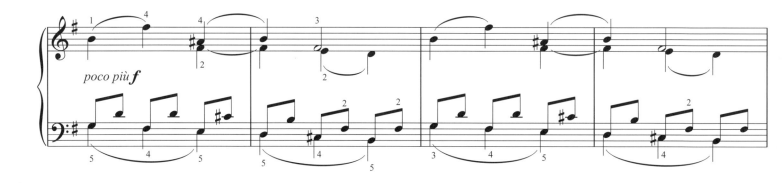

poco più *f*

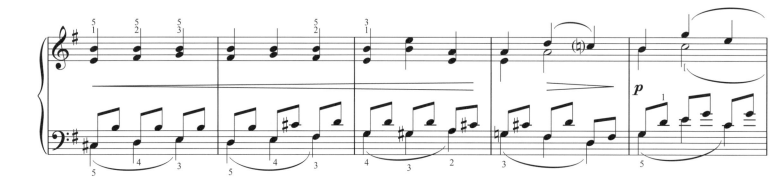

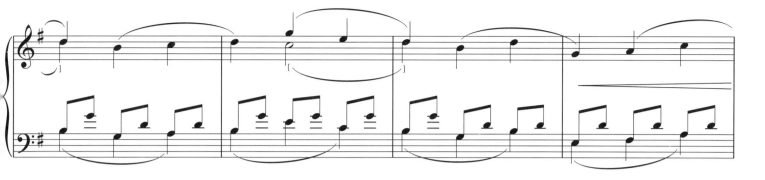

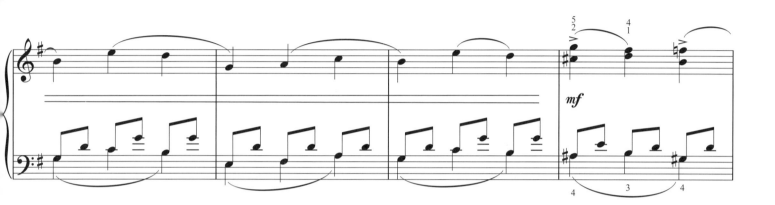

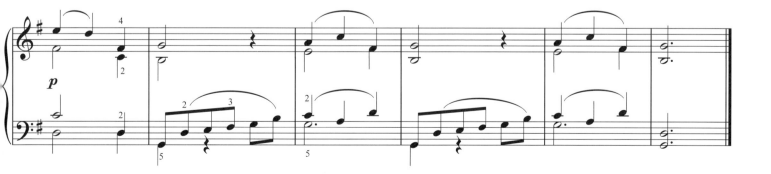

Dedicated to Volodja Davydov

Morning Prayer

from *Album for the Young*

Pyotr Il'yich Tchaikovsky
1840–1893
Op. 39, No. 1

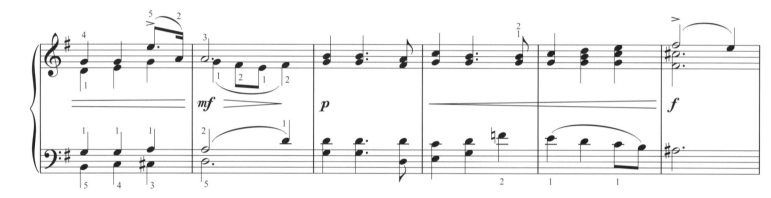

The Sick Doll
from *Album for the Young*

Pyotr Il'yich Tchaikovsky
1840–1893
Op. 39, No. 6

Moderate (𝅘𝅥 = 60-64)

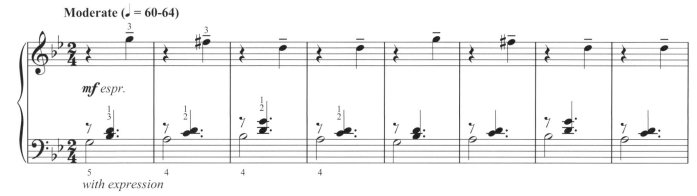

mf espr.

with expression

dim.

The Doll's Funeral
from *Album for the Young*

Pyotr Il'yich Tchaikovsky
1840–1893
Op. 39, No. 8

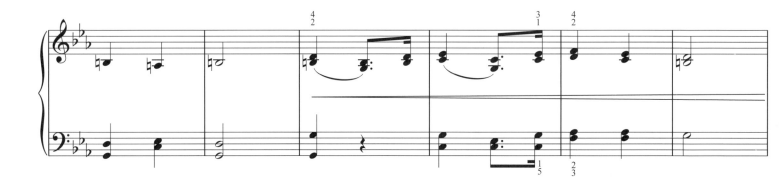

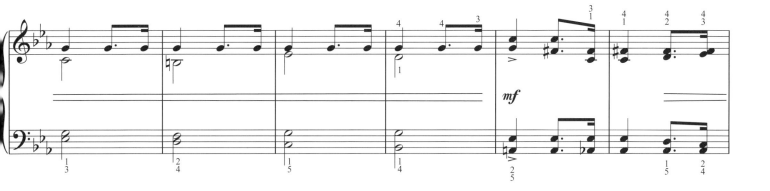

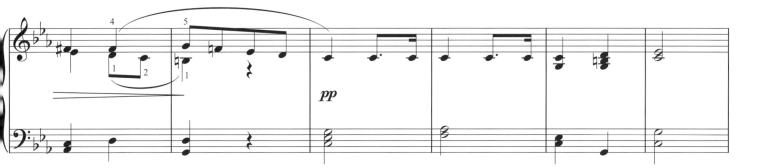

The New Doll

from *Album for the Young*

Pyotr Il'yich Tchaikovsky
1840–1893
Op. 39, No. 9

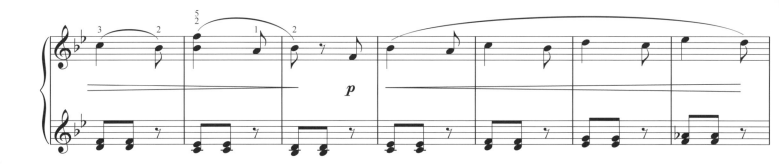

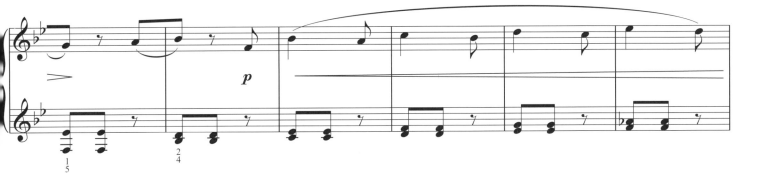

Italian Song
from *Album for the Young*

Pyotr Il'yich Tchaikovsky
1840–1893
Op. 39, No. 15

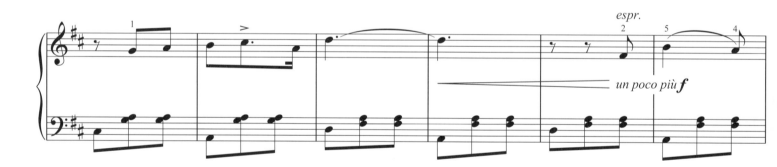

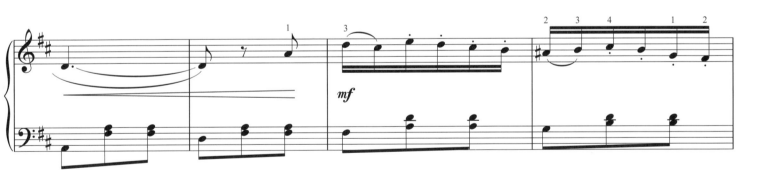

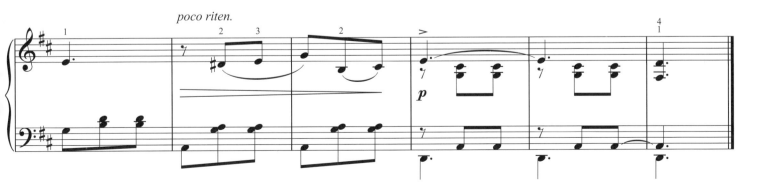

Old French Song

from *Album for the Young*

Pyotr Il'yich Tchaikovsky
1840–1893
Op. 39, No. 16

Very moderate (♩ = 68-72)
with feeling

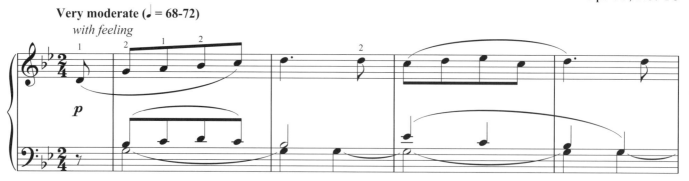

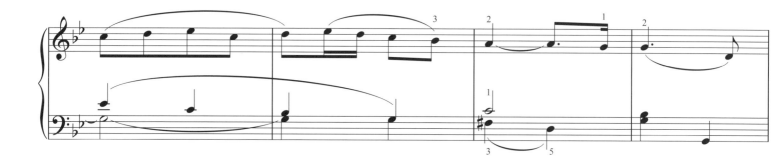

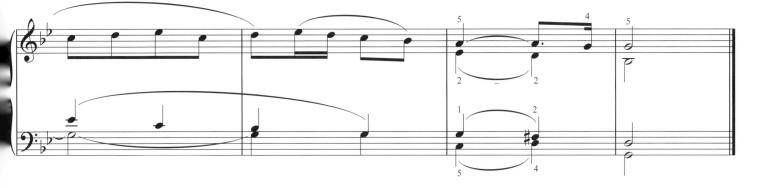

The Organ-Grinder Sings

from *Album for the Young*

Pyotr Il'yich Tchaikovsky
1840–1893
Op. 39, No. 24

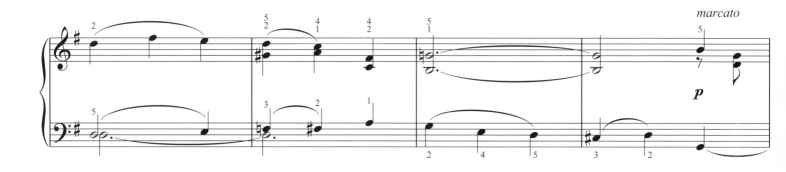

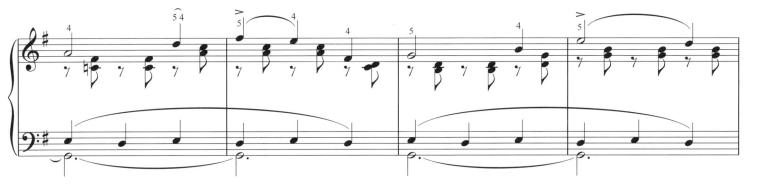

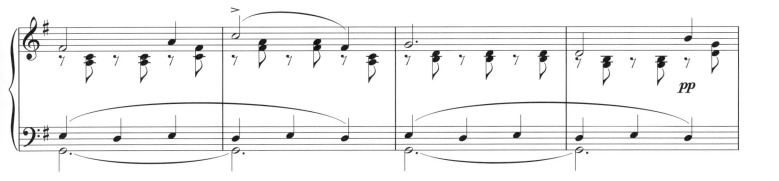

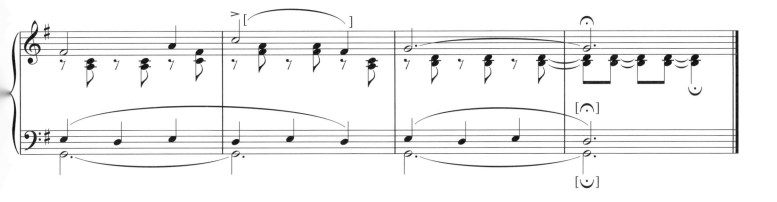

In Church

from *Album for the Young*

Pyotr Il'yich Tchaikovsky
1840–1893
Op. 39, No. 23

Moderate (♩ = 58–62)

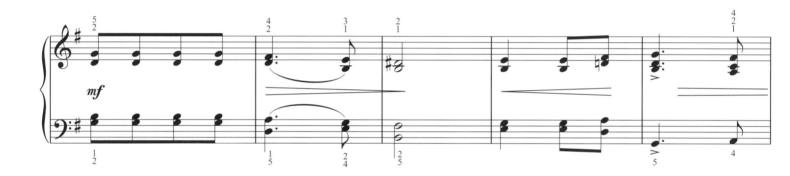

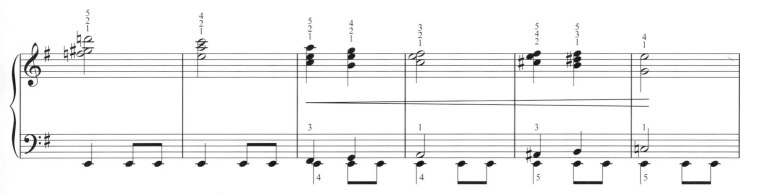

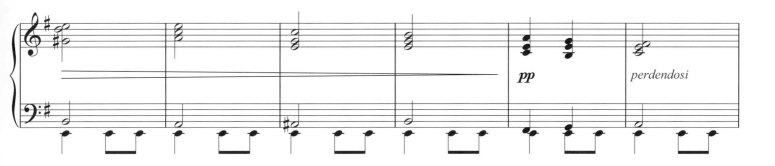

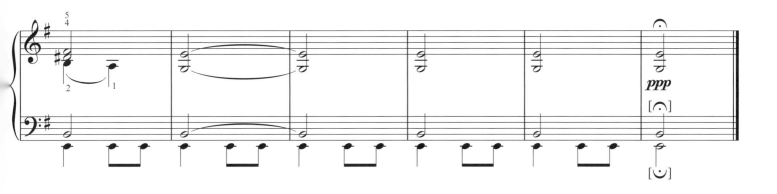

Sweet Dream
from *Album for the Young*

Pyotr Il'yich Tchaikovsky
1840–1893
Op. 39, No. 21

Moderate (♩ = 66–70)
with much feeling

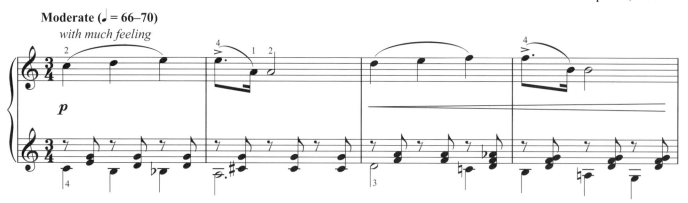

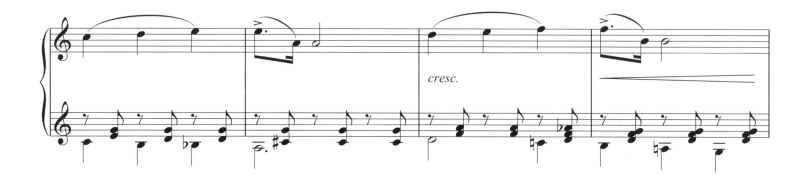

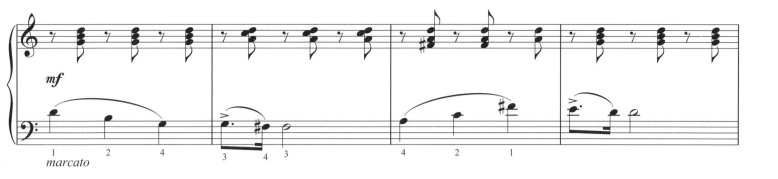

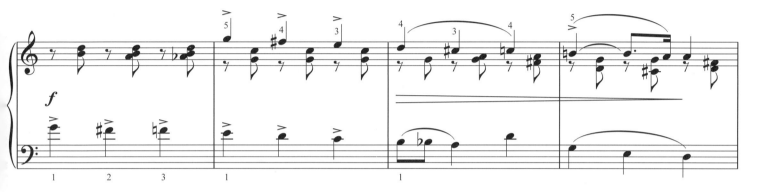

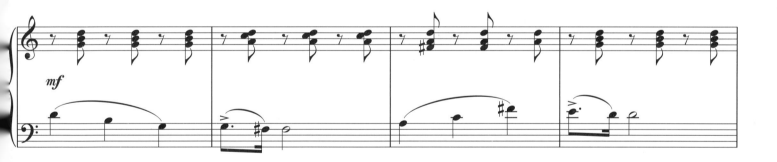

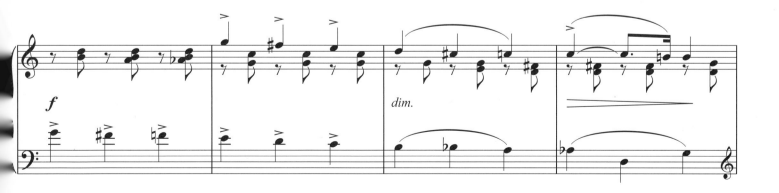

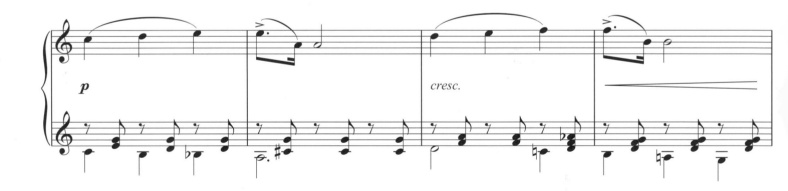

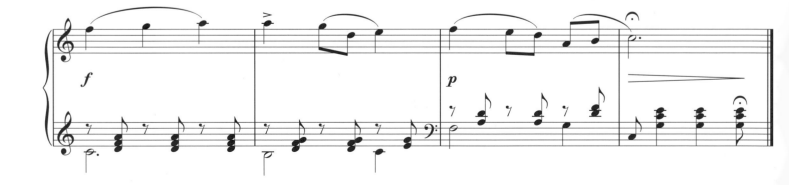